10

# DEADLIEST Predators

# Deadliest Snakes

Kris Hirschmann

ReferencePoint Press®

San Diego, CA

© 2017 ReferencePoint Press, Inc.
Printed in the United States

**For more information, contact:**
ReferencePoint Press, Inc.
PO Box 27779
San Diego, CA 92198
www.ReferencePointPress.com

LIBRARY OF CONGRESS CATALOGING-IN-PUBLICATION DATA

Names: Hirschmann, Kris, 1967-
Title: Deadliest snakes / by Kris Hirschmann.
Description: San Diego, CA : ReferencePoint Press, Inc., 2017. | Series: Deadliest predators series | Audience: Grade 7 to 8.- | Includes bibliographical references and index.
Identifiers: LCCN 2015046499 (print) | LCCN 2016007640 (ebook) | ISBN 9781682820568 (hardback) | ISBN 9781682820575 (epub)
Subjects: LCSH: Poisonous snakes--Juvenile literature.
Classification: LCC QL666.O6 H637 2017 (print) | LCC QL666.O6 (ebook) | DDC 597.96/165--dc23
LC record available at http://lccn.loc.gov/2015046499

# Contents

# Feared but Fascinating

When it comes to animals that scare people, snakes are close to the top of the list. Studies show that these creatures are second only to spiders in their fright factor. There is even a name for an excessive fear of snakes: ophidiophobia. People with this condition are so frightened by snakes that they cannot stand to see them on television or in photos, much less in real life. Hikes in the woods or even visits to local zoos are out of the question for these people, who arrange their whole lives just to avoid any possible snake contact.

This level of fear is not normal or rational, and most people do not feel this strongly. But many, many people have a less intense but still strong reaction to snakes. With their slithering, squirming, limbless bodies, glaring eyes, and potentially venomous fangs, snakes just make people shudder.

## A Real Danger

It is not surprising that people feel this way. There are about six hundred venomous snake species in the world. Some of them are so lethal that their bite can kill an adult human within hours. And even nonvenomous snakes can and do inflict painful bites if they are cornered or threatened.

The snake's prey has an even better reason to be afraid. Snakes are ruthless predators with all the tools they need to hunt, kill, and eat a wide variety of animals, including mammals, birds, amphibians, insects, and even other snakes. They are silent, strong, and deadly. When a hungry snake goes looking for food, all small creatures—and even some large ones, depending on the snake's size—are in grave danger.

## Nature in Balance

The snake's hunting abilities are undeniably intimidating. But snakes are not evil, and they do not hunt for fun. They hunt because they need to eat—and when they do, they help to maintain an ecosystem's natural balance. A snake that eats insects, for example, helps to keep bug populations from exploding out of control. A snake that eats rats keeps rodent populations in check.

A worker at a Florida dog kennel discovered this effect firsthand after he killed dozens of snakes he found living in the kennel's rafters. He was pleased to be rid of the pesky serpents—and so were the rats living in and around the kennel, which began to multiply out of control. "The rat population exploded," a state biologist reported later. "It took two years, hundreds of people-hours, and thousands of dollars to get control of the rats and repair the structural damage."[1]

This story is a good illustration of the snake's importance in nature's balance. Like all predators, snakes occupy an important niche in their home environments. If they are removed from the equation, the balance is disrupted. Unforeseen and often unpleasant developments are sure to follow.

*A deadly puff adder is milked for its venom. Many people fear snakes—and sometimes with good reason. But snakes also help maintain nature's balance and, increasingly, play an important role in medicine.*

## Medical Marvels

Snakes are not just good for pest control. They are also useful in the field of medicine, where snake venom is an effective treatment for many conditions. The primary use is to make medicine called antivenom or antivenin, which works as an antidote to snakebites. To make these substances, snake venom is injected in miniscule quantities into horses, which are large and strong enough to withstand the poison without any harm. The horses' bodies develop antibodies, which are proteins that have the ability to fight the venom. The antibodies are separated from the horses' blood and made into medicines that help snakebite victims to survive. Over its lifetime, one horse can safely generate and donate huge quantities of antibodies.

Antivenom is the substance most commonly produced from snake venom, but it is far from the only one. Many snake products are used to help sick people. A blood-clotting protein from one snake, for example, slows bleeding during surgery or after major trauma. The venom from a different snake breaks down life-threatening blood clots. Other substances from snakes are being explored as medicines for Parkinson's disease and cancer. Snake venom has even been used in skin creams that claim to reduce wrinkles and other signs of aging.

These applications and others help people on a daily basis—and medical research continues to explore the potential uses of snake venom. This substance is powerful, and it certainly has many uses that have not yet been discovered. Only time will tell how snakes and their venom may benefit people everywhere.

## Worthy of Respect

Understanding the benefits of snakes will not make people stop fearing them. Some snakes are, after all, potentially deadly. It would be foolish to approach or touch a snake without understanding the right way to do it or without knowing if the snake in question was venomous. So some level of concern is perfectly rational and could even be considered common sense for people who are not reptile experts.

Some scientists suggest, in fact, that a fear of snakes is actually built into the human gene pool. This fear would have been programmed into the earliest humans and strengthened over time until it reached a primal, uncontrollable level. "The idea is that throughout evolutionary history, humans that learned quickly to fear snakes could have been at an advantage to survive and reproduce," explains Vanessa LoBue, a scientist who studied this phenomenon. "Humans who detected the presence of snakes very quickly would have been more likely to pass on their genes."[2]

If LoBue and her colleagues are correct, snakes may have a scare factor that some people simply cannot withstand. But there is no rational reason for this fear to explode out of control, as it does in the case of ophidiophobia. Anyone can have a healthy respect for these reptiles and stay out of their way but still enjoy them — from a safe distance. And if people choose, they can learn more about snakes and gain the knowledge and the confidence to get closer. By understanding these remarkable creatures, they can safely give them the admiration they so richly deserve.

# Chapter 1

# Inland Taipan

Some snake venoms are more potent than others. In studying these differences, scientists have learned that the inland taipan of Australia slithers straight to the top of the pile. Also known as the small-scaled snake or the fierce snake, this creature has by far the deadliest venom of any snake on Earth. The toxins delivered in a single bite could kill up to 250,000 small rodents—which is equal to about one hundred very unlucky adult humans. With this impressive killing power, the inland taipan poses a mortal danger to anyone who enters its range.

## Body Basics

The inland taipan's rather plain body gives no hint about the danger lurking inside. This reptile is slightly but not remarkably large for a snake—adults are usually about 5 to 6 feet (1.5 to 1.8 m) long, which is similar to an adult human's height. Individuals do sometimes grow longer, up to a maximum of more than 8 feet (2.4 m), but shorter lengths are more typical. The build is medium, neither slender nor thick, although it tends a bit toward the stocky side. The snake's head is rectangular in shape, but not strongly so, and it is about the same width as the rest of the body.

The inland taipan's color depends on the time of year. During warm seasons, the snake's small scales are tan to olive with blackish edges. The way the scales align creates dark V-shaped marks on the snake's body. During cold seasons, the snake's scales darken to a deep brown all over. The smooth head is darker than the body, ranging from dark brown during the summer to a shiny black during the winter. The round eyes are medium size and a deep brownish black.

Inside the taipan's mouth are the snake's deadly fangs. Like all members of the Elapidae family, the inland taipan has fixed fangs, which means they stay in the same position all the time. The fangs are short, only .25 to .5 inches (.6 to 1.3 cm) long, and they are hollow. They work like hypodermic needles to inject venom into the flesh of the snake's prey.

## Home and Habits

The inland taipan lives and hunts in a remote part of central Australia. In this semiarid region, known as the black soil plains, the climate is hot and dry most of the time. Plant life is sparse, and the ground is dry and cracked. It is a hostile environment—but the inland taipan manages not only to survive but also to thrive here. Although good population counts do not exist, scientists believe that the inland taipan is plentiful in its home territory.

There are a couple of reasons why these snakes are so hard to count. The remoteness of the inland taipan's range is one reason. Additionally, these snakes seldom emerge during the midday and evening hours. They are active only in the early morning, before the day gets too hot. As the sun rises and the black soil plains start

*The inland taipan, whose scale colors change with the seasons, has the deadliest venom of any snake on Earth. A single bite packs enough toxins to kill up to 250,000 small rodents or one hundred humans.*

to bake in the bright sunlight, the snakes retreat into deep cracks and abandoned rodent burrows. They rest through the heat of the day and all through the night. At the first light of dawn, they rouse themselves for another burst of outdoor activity.

## On the Hunt

Most of this activity involves hunting. The inland taipan slithers over and through the cracked ground looking for

# THE INLAND TAIPAN
## AT A GLANCE

- Scientific name: Oxyuranus microlepidotus
- Scientific family: Elapidae
- Range: Central east Australia
- Habitat: Black soil plains in dry regions
- Average size: 6 feet (2 m)
- Diet: Small rodents
- Life span: Up to twenty years
- Key features: Small, smooth scales
- Deadly because: Most toxic venom of any snake
- Conservation status: Least concern

rats, mice, and other small mammals to eat. It will occasionally eat a bird if no other prey is available, but this is not a favorite meal.

The inland taipan's hunting patterns vary depending on the season. During certain times of the year, rat and mouse populations explode on the black soil plains. The snakes take full advantage of this bonanza. They hunt and eat often, and their bodies become thicker and heavier. When rodent populations subside, so does the inland taipan's activity level. The snake hunts and eats less, and it becomes thinner. It rests to save its energy until rodent populations rise once again.

Whether it is a time of feast or famine, the inland taipan's hunting techniques stay the same. The snake moves quickly across its territory searching for prey. It looks around with its keen eyes, searching for the slightest hint of motion. It also flicks its tongue in and out. The tongue collects scent particles from the air and deposits them in the snake's scent organ, which is located on the roof of the mouth.

As soon as the inland taipan sees or smells prey, the hunt is on. The snake makes no attempt to hide or to ambush its intended victim. It simply follows the animal into the ground and chases it through the maze of underground cracks. Sooner or later the rodent finds itself backed into a corner with nowhere to run.

When this happens, the inland taipan seizes its chance. It opens its mouth, bares its needle-sharp fangs,

*Rats (such as this Australia native) and other small mammals are a favorite meal for the inland taipan. To kill its prey it strikes repeatedly with its needle-sharp fangs.*

and strikes repeatedly—up to eight times in a row. With each strike, the snake plunges its fangs into the prey's flesh and injects up to 100 milligrams of venom. The venom goes to work with lightning speed to immobilize the prey, which is then gulped down whole, headfirst, by its hungry attacker.

## Vicious Venom

Scientists have studied the venom of the inland taipan to learn why it is so lethal. The answer lies in the fact that this snake's venom includes a mixture of poisons with different effects. Some of these poisons, for instance, work to paralyze the central nervous system. Others affect the blood and muscles. Still others affect the kidneys and the blood vessels. To top it all off, the venom also contains a substance that helps the body quickly absorb these poisons.

This cocktail of toxins has a dramatic effect on the inland taipan's victims. It overwhelms the snake's typical small targets almost instantly. Larger targets, such as humans, do not succumb quite as quickly—but the effects are felt immediately. The victim develops a splitting headache, nausea, abdominal pain, and dizziness as the venom spreads throughout the body. The muscles weaken, and breathing becomes difficult. "Effectively what it will do is it will start shutting down the function of messages going to your brain, to your vital organs, your lungs and your heart and even your muscles,"[3] explains Julie Mendezona, head reptile keeper at the Australian Reptile Park near Sydney, Australia.

Once this shutdown begins, it is hard to stop. The symptoms progress until the bite victim becomes com-

# QUICK KILLER

**Most venomous snakes strike their prey once, then back off. They bide their time, watching and waiting as their victim gets weaker and weaker. Only when the prey is too sick to struggle does the snake move in for a meal.**

**The inland taipan has a different technique. Its venom is so devastatingly powerful that it paralyzes mice and rats almost instantly. The inland taipan is therefore able to trap and hold prey with its body without being bitten or scratched. It may wrap itself around a rodent and strike repeatedly, driving its venom deep into the prey's body.**

**The venom load delivered in multiple bites is enough to kill hundreds of thousands of rodents. This amount of killing power might seem excessive, but it is an adaptation that helps the inland taipan to survive. By subduing its prey quickly, this snake manages to thrive in a sparse and challenging habitat.**

pletely paralyzed. At this point convulsions, organ failure, and death are not far behind. From beginning to end, the whole process might take as little as forty-five minutes.

These facts are bad enough on their own. But there is yet another reason to fear the inland taipan. Most venomous snakes deliver a high percentage of so-called dry bites, or bites that do not inject venom. The inland taipan, however, injects venom 100 percent of the time. This means that no one gets lucky when attacked by this reptile. Each and every time it occurs, the bite of the inland taipan is a life-threatening emergency.

# Deadly but Calm

Thankfully for the human population, such emergencies are rare. This is partly because the inland taipan lives in remote areas where people seldom go. But it is also partly due to the inland taipan's personality. This snake is calm and nonaggressive, and it would much rather hide than fight. If people do enter its territory, it will lie still and let them pass if it does not feel endangered.

Like any animal, though, the inland taipan will defend itself if it feels angry or afraid. If a person corners or threatens an inland taipan, the snake responds by curling itself tightly. It raises the front part of its body in a tight S shape with the head pointing directly toward the intruder. This position is called a threat display. It is the snake's way of showing its alarm and telling visitors to back off—now.

If a person ignores this message and comes too close, the snake will launch itself forward in attack, using its tightly coiled body like a spring. It is quick and accurate. It can complete a strike and inject its venom within a fraction of a second. It then slithers away to safety before the human victim even realizes what is happening.

A handful of people have been attacked in this way over the years. Incredibly, though, all known human victims have survived thanks to prompt treatment with antivenom, a medicine that counteracts the inland taipan's toxins. Some victims have experienced lasting effects, including heart and muscle problems, from the inland taipan's bite. But at least they are alive.

In terms of its deadly potential, then, the inland taipan is the worst of the worst—but it poses little real threat to people. As one snake expert says, "Sure, it has lethal

*A professional snake handler grasps an inland taipan. Although its bite is deadly, it is not an aggressive snake; it would rather hide than fight.*

venom with the potential to kill humans, but there is a world of difference between potentiality and reality. The inland taipan is the world's most venomous snake . . . but is by far NOT the world's deadliest snake."[4] It is a lucky break for the human population that this lethal reptile prefers to keep its distance.

# Chapter 2

# Black Mamba

Over two hundred different species of snakes lurk in the wild heart of Africa. Of these, the most feared by far is the black mamba—and this reputation is well deserved. The black mamba is notoriously venomous, aggressive, and ill-tempered. It slithers with terrifying speed, fast enough to overtake a fleeing person. It injects venom with virtually every bite. And worst of all, this deadly creature's home range overlaps with human communities, so it comes into fairly frequent contact with potential victims.

With all of these deadly characteristics, the black mamba is widely considered to be the world's most dangerous snake. People who receive the mamba's kiss of death, as this snake's bite is often called, are unlikely to survive the encounter.

## Body Basics

The black mamba is not actually black. Its body ranges from olive brown to gray or sometimes light tan, with a pale yellow to cream-colored belly. This snake gets its name from the inside of its mouth, which is inky black in color. Even the snake's forked tongue is black. Two needle-sharp fangs, each up to .75 inches (2 cm) long, are found at the front of the mouth. The head is often described as being coffin shaped—a suitable description considering this snake's killing power. The eyes are round, medium in size, and dark brown in the center, with pale yellow rings along the outer edges.

In terms of its overall build, the black mamba's body is rounded, with a tapering tail, and it is frighteningly long. This snake's average length is about 8 to 9 feet (2.5 to 3 m), but some individuals are much bigger. The largest recorded black mamba was nearly 15 feet (4.5 m) long, or about the length of a car, making this reptile Africa's longest venomous snake and the world's second longest, after the king cobra.

Despite its intimidating length, the black mamba is not bulky. This snake has a slender build that makes it surprisingly lightweight for its length. Even the longest black mambas usually weigh less than 4 pounds (1.8 kg). This slim, light frame lets the black mamba slither easily across tree branches, slip into cracks and crevices, or travel anywhere else it wants to go.

## Home and Habits

Black mambas are found across a large part of southeastern Africa. They have been occasionally reported in western Africa as well, although scientists have not confirmed these sightings. Within their known range, black mambas are fairly common and in no danger of extinction.

Black mambas are found in dry regions and are mostly ground dwellers. They prefer low, open areas such as savannas, but may settle in woodlands and forests as well. They are sometimes found in hilly areas at higher altitudes, up to a maximum of about 6,000 feet (1,829 m), but this is much less common. Wherever it settles, a black mamba creates a lair inside a safe, enclosed spot, such as an old termite mound, an abandoned animal burrow, or a rocky crevice. It will live in this lair for a long period, perhaps even for years, if its environment is not disturbed and it is able to find enough food.

Black mambas stick to their lairs during the nighttime hours. They emerge during the daytime, when the sunlight can warm their bodies. They are sometimes seen basking on rocks before the day becomes too hot. Occasionally they may also climb into trees and rest on high branches. Climbing behavior is more common among young black mambas, which are smaller and more vulnerable to ground-dwelling predators. Slithering into treetops helps them to stay safe as they grow and develop.

## On the Hunt

A big part of the black mamba's day is devoted to hunting. This snake eats mostly small mammals, such as rock hyrax (furry, rodent-like creatures about the size of guinea pigs), bush babies, and bats. It will also eat birds or other snakes.

The black mamba is an ambush hunter. This means that instead of chasing prey, it settles into a hidden area and stays very still. It patiently watches and waits. If the snake is lucky, a small animal will eventually wander too close. When this happens, the black mamba reacts with lightning speed. It lunges into the open, its black mouth gaping to expose its sharp fangs. It buries these fangs in the prey's body and injects a killing dose of venom.

When the strike is complete, the black mamba pulls back to a safe distance, where it will not be bitten or

*The black mamba (pictured) is aggressive, bad-tempered, and lightning fast. Because its habitat overlaps with human communities, this highly venomous snake represents a grave threat to people.*

scratched. It watches the prey as the venom, which is loaded with deadly neurotoxins, takes effect. The prey starts to lose control of its body as the brain and nerves shut down and the muscles stop working. The snake follows the rapidly weakening animal if it tries to escape and strikes again, if necessary, to inject more venom. It varies this technique just a bit when it comes to small

# THE BLACK MAMBA
## AT A GLANCE

- **Scientific name:** *Dendroaspis polylepis*
- **Scientific family: Elapidae**
- **Range: Southern and eastern Africa**
- **Habitat: Savannas, woodlands, and forests**
- **Average size: 8 to 9 feet (2 to 3 m)**
- **Diet: Small birds and mammals**
- **Life span: Up to eleven years**
- **Key features: Black inner mouth**
- **Deadly because: Fast and aggressive**
- **Conservation status: Least concern**

birds, which can fly away. In these cases the black mamba clamps its jaws tightly, using its teeth to hold its prey until the unfortunate animal stops struggling.

When the prey finally collapses, paralyzed, the black mamba moves in at last to enjoy its meal. The snake usually swallows its prey headfirst and whole. An especially large meal can create a visible lump in the black mamba's body. The lump disappears quickly, though, as the mamba digests its food. These snakes can completely digest a small animal in eight to ten hours. After the prey has been absorbed, the snake is ready to hunt once again.

## Defensive Display

Despite their fearsome reputation, black mambas do not use their ambush techniques on people. They would rather slither away, unnoticed, than attack. As one snake catcher explains, "Mambas . . . are very secretive. They don't want to be stopped or confronted. They're extremely nervous and alert and they'll be gone at the slightest hint of danger." However, he cautions, "they'll be aggressive in a very small area."[5] These snakes are known to be fearless if cornered or threatened, during

*The gaping mouth of a black mamba reveals a black interior. After injecting a paralyzing dose of venom into its prey, the snake often pulls back and waits to eat until the prey can no longer move.*

# A SPEEDY SNAKE

When it comes to speed, the black mamba is the undisputed champion of the snake world. Many sources claim that this reptile's top speed is about 12 miles per hour (19 km/h). Some experts believe that this is an exaggeration and that the real number is closer to 10 miles per hour (16 km/h). But either way, it is fast. In the open, a person could probably outrun a black mamba in full slither—but this snake is not usually encountered in the open. It lurks in areas full of bushes, trees, and undergrowth that prevent top running speeds. The black mamba could easily overtake a fleeing human in these conditions.

Luckily for its potential victims, the black mamba uses its frightening speed mostly to escape from danger, not to attack. If cornered, though, the snake can and will do anything necessary to protect itself—and it will do it quickly. No one is safe when the black mamba puts its terrifying speed to work.

breeding season, or when defending their territory. They will also become aggressive toward anyone or anything that blocks the path to their lair.

It is not hard to tell when a black mamba is upset. An angry mamba turns to face any threat head-on. It raises the front one-third of its body off the ground and spreads the skin of its neck slightly to make itself seem larger. It opens its black mouth wide and hisses. It may even move toward the intruder in this position. Extremely upset black mambas have been known to move forward with their heads and bodies raised high above the ground. It is a terrifying sight and one that signals the gravest danger for the object of the snake's fury.

If an intruder ignores these signs and fails to flee, the snake takes bold action. It thrusts itself forward and upward to strike. Because its head is already 3 to 4 feet (.9 to 1.2 m) off the ground at this point, the black mamba is capable of burying its fangs in a person's chest or head—perilously close to the vital organs.

No matter where it lands, the black mamba's bite is potentially lethal, delivering up to 400 milligrams of venom. This is enough to kill dozens of adult humans. Even worse, though, is the fact that this snake can strike multiple times in a row, up to an incredible twelve times in a single second. The attack happens so quickly that a person may think he or she was only bitten once. But the many puncture wounds left on the victim's skin reveal the deadly truth.

## The Kiss of Death

Once a person has been bitten, the clock is ticking. The black mamba's venom is extremely fast acting and spreads rapidly through the person's system. The first symptoms, which include dizziness, headache, a racing heart, and breathing trouble, appear within fifteen to thirty minutes. Convulsions, paralysis, and unconsciousness soon follow. The symptoms progress until the victim dies of suffocation or heart collapse, generally between seven and fifteen hours after the bite occurs.

In some instances, though, the process can be much faster. A particularly gruesome case occurred in March 2008, when a British student was bitten by a black mamba at a safari guide training school in Hoedspruit,

*A black mamba feeds after capturing a rodent. Like all snakes, it swallows its prey whole.*

South Africa. Nathan Layton was helping to capture a black mamba that had roamed into the school when he was struck on the index finger. Not realizing what had happened, Layton continued on to class. But thirty minutes later he started to feel ill. He whispered to his instructor that his vision had gone blurry—and things happened very quickly from that point on. "A few seconds after he said this, he collapsed," the instructor recalls. "He was breathing very shallow and started gasping for air."[6] Within an hour of being bitten, Layton was dead of heart failure.

Layton's death may have been unusually quick, but the speed was the only unusual aspect of the situation. Even with prompt antivenom treatment, many black mamba victims die—and without it, the picture is unrelentingly grim. The black mamba's bite is thought to be 100 percent fatal without treatment.

This is bad news in rural Africa, where medical facilities are few and far between and antivenom is not easily available. In these areas, the only real protection against the black mamba is staying away from it—preferably far, far away. Anyone who gets too close to the world's most dangerous snake is flirting with death.

# Chapter 3

# Saw-Scaled Viper

A snake's ranking on the venom scale does not have much to do with its overall danger to the human population. If a certain type of snake kills 100 percent of its human bite victims, but it only bites a few people per year, it is not considered to be a real threat. On the other hand, a snake that kills a smaller percentage of its victims, but bites often, can take a serious toll on its human neighbors.

This is the case with the saw-scaled viper, a serpent that is believed to cause more human deaths each year worldwide than any other snake. Untreated, the saw-scaled viper's bite kills about 10 to 20 percent of its victims. If treated, this number falls to less than 1 percent. However, the saw-scaled viper is common in human-inhabited areas where incomes are low and access to health care is limited. This fact, combined with the saw-scaled viper's legendary aggressiveness and bad temper, leads to frequent bites—hundreds of thousands per year—and these encounters cause more than twenty thousand documented human deaths annually. As far as people are concerned, the saw-scaled viper is the deadliest snake on Earth.

## Body Basics

The saw-scaled viper is a fairly small snake. The average length is about 1 foot (.3 m) long. The biggest individuals may reach lengths of 2 feet (.6 m), but vipers of this size are rare.

Although the saw-scaled viper is short, it is stocky. Its body is rounded and thick, with a back end that tapers quickly into a pointed tail. At the front is the triangular head, which is markedly wider than the neck. The head is dominated by two large, perfectly circular eyes, which are mostly tan with black, vertical slits for pupils. The top

*Dominating the head of the saw-scaled viper (pictured) are two large, perfectly round eyes with vertical slits for pupils. The saw-scaled viper is believed to cause more human deaths than any other snake.*

of the head bears a white cross-shaped mark, a distinctive feature that makes this snake easy to identify.

In terms of color, the saw-scaled viper is patterned in shades of black, dark brown, tan, and white. The reptile's back is barred, alternating between narrow white bars and broader brown bars. Wavy white lines run down the sides of the body. The belly is predominantly white, with dark brown or blackish spots on the scales.

On all parts of its body, the saw-scaled viper looks dull and dry rather than shiny, like many snakes. The dry appearance comes from the snake's rough scales, which are keeled, meaning they have a raised ridge in the center. The keels on some of the scales are serrated. This means their top edges are jagged, like knives. The jagged edges are too small to see at a glance, but they break up the scales' surfaces and give the snake its overall dry look.

## Home and Habits

The saw-scaled viper's colors and dryness both serve as camouflage. This snake is found from northern Africa through the Middle East and into India, where deserts and semiarid habitats are common. It strongly prefers sandy, rocky areas that are dotted with sparse grass and scrubby bushes. With its desert-tone colors, the saw-scaled viper blends perfectly into its surroundings.

This camouflage comes in handy on cool days, when the snake may emerge during the daytime and is more likely to be seen. Most of the time, though, the saw-scaled viper hides during the daytime hours to avoid the blistering desert heat. In hilly areas, it takes shelter under tumbled rocks or inside caves and cracks. In flatter re-

- **Scientific name:** *Echis carinatus*
- **Scientific family:** Viperidae
- **Range:** Northern Africa, Middle East, and India
- **Habitat:** Deserts and dry scrubland
- **Average size:** 1 foot (.3 m)
- **Diet:** Rodents, lizards, frogs, insects
- **Life span:** More than twenty years
- **Key features:** Rough scales with serrated central ridges
- **Deadly because:** Lives in populated areas and bites often
- **Conservation status:** Least concern

gions, it rests beneath hedges, scrub, and piles of dead leaves. Sometimes it even buries itself in sand, leaving just its slit eyes poking out to observe its surroundings.

When the sun sets and the ground cools down, the saw-scaled viper emerges from its hiding place. It is alert, active—and hungry. It is ready to look for food.

## On the Hunt

The saw-scaled viper is not a picky eater. It will take almost any kind of prey it can get, including small rodents, lizards, frogs, and insects. Other snakes are sometimes eaten as well, although this is a less common meal.

Because saw-scaled vipers cannot slither quickly, they do not attempt to chase prey. Instead, they are ambush hunters. They find a good hiding place and settle down to wait. They look around with their sharp eyes. They flick their forked tongues in and out to detect the scent of possible prey. They can also feel vibrations through the ground with their bodies. These vibrations alert them when small animals are moving nearby.

*Wavy lines and alternating shades of black, brown, and white provide camouflage for the saw-scaled viper (pictured). These colors and patterns help it to blend into the sandy, rocky, arid regions that are its home.*

As a potential meal approaches, the viper prepares to strike. It waits, muscles tense, as the prey comes closer and closer. The prey must come within about two-thirds of the snake's body length to be in striking range.

When the animal crosses this deadly threshold, the snake lunges. It opens its mouth wide as it darts toward its prey. Simultaneously the snake's long fangs, which are normally folded backward and tucked into the roof of the mouth, swing forward and outward on bony hinges. By the time the mouth is fully open, the fangs have shifted into full attack position and point straight at the target like two tiny daggers. Hinged fangs, which are a feature of all vipers, are typically much longer than the fixed fangs of the Elapidae family. They can therefore plunge deeper into a victim's flesh.

Mouth wide open and fangs exposed, the viper crosses the distance to its prey in a fraction of a second, moving much too quickly to see—or to avoid. It sinks its hollow fangs into the prey and uses them like hypodermic needles to inject a lethal dose of venom. Then it backs off and waits for the poison to take effect. When the prey collapses, the viper moves in to swallow its meal.

## Potent Venom

The saw-scaled viper's venom contains mostly poisons that affect the circulatory system. These substances spread quickly through the prey's bloodstream. They go to work breaking down the animal's blood cells and blood vessels. The bite victim starts to bleed internally as its circulatory system springs countless leaks. The

# SIDEWINDING

Although saw-scaled vipers can and often do slither in a straight line, they use a method called sidewinding to make their way across sand dunes and other loose surfaces. A sidewinding snake throws its head sideways. The rest of the body follows in an arc that does not touch the ground. This means that at one moment, the snake's head and tail may be touching the ground while the central body is airborne. As it travels, the snake leaves a distinctive trail that looks like a series of straight, parallel lines.

Sidewinding is not unique to saw-scaled vipers. Many desert snakes use this method of travel, which has two major advantages over slithering. First, sidewinding is faster and more efficient in sand, which does not provide a solid surface for the snake's scales to grab. Second, it reduces the amount of time the snake's belly is in direct contact with the blistering ground. The snake's body cools a tiny bit each time it is raised, preventing the snake from overheating in its desert home.

leaks cause the blood pressure to drop dramatically, and the heart cannot keep up. Without enough blood to pump, it falters and then fails.

A person who is bitten by a saw-scaled viper is much larger than the snake's typical prey. The venom load is therefore less in relation to body weight and works more slowly than it would in a smaller creature. However, the saw-scaled viper can deliver enough venom to kill a human—up to double the necessary amount—

and the victim will experience many unpleasant effects as the process unfolds.

The first symptom of a saw-scaled viper bite is excruciating pain at the injection site. The bitten area starts to swell and blister within minutes. The swelling spreads, and within twelve to twenty-four hours an entire arm or leg can be affected. By this time the flesh around the bite is starting to blacken and die.

Internally, the bite victim is in serious trouble. The blood is thinning and has lost its ability to coagulate. The victim may start bleeding from the eyes, mouth, ears, and other mucous membranes as tiny blood vessels rupture. Meanwhile, the kidneys are working frantically to remove poisons and broken cells from the blood—but they are fighting a losing battle. They collapse under the strain. Heart failure and death soon follow.

## A Bad Temper

This scenario is all too common in areas where the saw-scaled viper lives. This snake comes into frequent contact with humans, and it is notoriously ill-tempered. It will strike at the slightest provocation. It has even been known to chase people when particularly irritated. As one expert says, "A saw-scaled viper is like a loaded gun with a hair trigger." After being called to capture one of these snakes in a person's home, he recalls, "In the car driving away it was jumping in the box on my wife's knee. We got it home and put it in a tank and it was striking the glass to get at me. It was really feisty."[7]

Luckily, the saw-scaled viper does warn people when it is upset, if it has the chance. The snake coils its body around itself in loops, keeping its head point-

*A saw-scaled viper is milked for its venom. The poisons in the snake's venom mainly affect the circulatory system—causing excruciating pain, swelling, and internal bleeding.*

ing at a threatening person. It slides its body around continually in a way that makes the serrated scales rub against each other. This action produces a distinct rustling or windy noise. To add to the effect, the snake opens its mouth and hisses loudly. This threat display is spectacular—and usually effective. Anyone who sees it would be wise to back off immediately.

But people do not always get the chance to back off. In the saw-scaled viper's home range, it is common for people to walk around outdoors with little or no foot protection. These people are sometimes bitten without warning after stepping on or near a snake. Saw-scaled vipers are also known to curl up near people's houses, in or under anything that provides shelter. They will lash out at any unsuspecting human who disturbs their rest.

People who live in areas where they are likely to encounter saw-scaled vipers know all about this snake's lethal potential. They know that they could die without immediate medical attention. With prompt treatment, they can dramatically improve their chances of survival—but where this serpent is concerned, there are no guarantees. As the world's top human-killing snake, the saw-scaled viper has proven fatal to countless people over the centuries, and it will continue to claim victims in the years yet to come.

# Chapter 4

# King Cobra

The thickly forested areas of Southeast Asia, India, and southern China are home to the king cobra, a fearsome reptile that is by far the world's longest venomous snake. This giant's venom is not the most potent in the snake kingdom—but anything it lacks in power, it makes up in quantity. The king cobra injects more venom with each bite than any other snake in the world, flooding its victims' systems with more than enough poison to cause a quick and painful death.

This fact alone would qualify the king cobra for a spot on any deadliest snakes list. Even worse, though, is the fact that this snake's range and hunting habits bring it into frequent contact with humans. Attacks therefore can and do occur regularly. Many people die each year following encounters with this terrifying serpent.

## Body Basics

At first glance, the king cobra's large size is its most striking feature. This intimidating creature averages about 13 feet (4 m) in length. However, some individuals grow to lengths exceeding 18 feet (5.5 m). This is about as long as three adult humans lying end to end. The body is rounded, with a prominent spinal ridge along the back, and the build is slender. Even the largest king cobras weigh in somewhere between 15 to 20 pounds (7 to 9 kg)—not very heavy for a creature of such size.

The king cobra's small scales glisten in sunlight, giving this snake a shiny appearance. The color and patterns vary depending on the location and habitat. The snake's back can be tan, brown, black, or olive green. It may be either solid or banded with lighter stripes. The belly is pale yellow to cream color, with broad horizontal scales.

More broad scales cover the king cobra's head, which is powerful and wedge shaped. The eyes are round, with deep black pupils surrounded by a yellow ring. When the snake opens its large mouth, it exposes its forked, dark-colored tongue and its curved, .5-inch-long (1.27 cm) fangs, which are fixed at the front of the mouth.

## Home and Habits

The king cobra is widespread across a large area of Asia, from India eastward through southern China and southward to the Philippines, Malaysia, and Indonesia. This snake is a good climber and is most often found in areas with plenty of trees, shrubs, and undergrowth that it can slither over and through. It is also an excellent swimmer and prefers to live near standing water bodies, such as ponds and lakes.

The king cobra usually rests during the nighttime hours. Rather than curling into a ball, it often stretches its long body out. Fallen logs and dead vegetation are favorite hiding places, and abandoned animal burrows may be used as well. In human-inhabited areas, king cobras sometimes enter homes, and they may take shelter in a dark, cozy basement or attic.

When daytime arrives, a king cobra emerges from its resting spot. It heads straight for a sunny spot and spends some time basking to warm its body. It may climb high into a tree to find a safe perch for this activity. The snake will rest quietly until its body temperature climbs to a comfortable level. When it feels warm enough, the snake begins its daily rounds.

*The king cobra (pictured) tastes the air with its dark, forked tongue. Its most distinctive feature, when threatened, is a flared hood, but its eyes— with deep black pupils ringed in yellow—add to its menacing look.*

# THE KING COBRA AT A GLANCE

- Scientific name: *Ophiophagus hannah*
- Scientific family: Elapidae
- Range: Southeast Asia, including India, China, the Philippines, Malaysia, and Indonesia
- Habitat: Dense forests with lakes, ponds, and streams
- Length: Up to 18 feet (6 m)
- Diet: Mostly snakes; sometimes small birds or mammals
- Life span: Up to twenty years
- Key features: Size and spreading neck flap, or hood
- Deadly because: Venom quantity
- Conservation status: Vulnerable

## On the Hunt

Like most snakes, the king cobra spends the majority of its active time looking for its next meal. It hunts and eats mostly other snakes. In fact, the first part of the king cobra's scientific name, *Ophiophagus*, means "snake eater." It particularly enjoys rat snakes and often lurks in rat-infested areas—not to catch the rats but rather to hunt their predators. If rat snakes are not available, the king cobra will eat just about any kind of snake, including other king cobras. If a snake meal cannot be found, the king cobra will take small rodents, birds, or lizards as a last resort.

Whatever prey it pursues, the king cobra is an active hunter that seeks prey rather than hiding in ambush. This snake glides smoothly through underbrush, tree branches, and loose leaves. It swims stealthily across bodies of water. It looks around with its keen eyes as it travels, spotting the slightest motion more than 300 feet (91 m) away. It tastes the air with its forked tongue, seeking scent trails that will lead it to food, and it also listens carefully to its surroundings. King cobras have no ears, but they "hear" with their bodies, which detect the sound vibrations of nearby creatures.

When the king cobra detects prey, it silently draws near. Eventually it gets close enough to strike—and it does so with dizzying speed. The king cobra sinks its fangs into the prey's body and injects up to an astonishing 1.4 teaspoons (7 milliliters) of venom. It draws back a short distance and waits while the prey weakens. When the prey can no longer struggle—but while it is still very much alive—the king cobra moves in and swallows the animal whole.

## The Response to Threats

Like most snakes, king cobras avoid direct contact with humans if at all possible. In fact, even though these snakes often live near people, they manage to stay hidden most of the time—proof of their basically calm nature. As one expert points out, "If the snake were really habitually aggressive, records of its bite would be frequent; as it is, they are extremely rare."[8]

But despite the king cobra's secretive nature, contact with people is sometimes unavoidable. When it occurs, the snake's first instinct is to slither away. If the king co-

*A king cobra devours another snake. To catch its prey, the king cobra glides smoothly through brush, branches, and leaves until it picks up the scent and vibrations that signal the presence of food.*

bra feels cornered or threatened, though, it stages one of nature's most frightening defensive displays in an effort to protect itself.

The snake begins its display by raising the front one-third of its body off the ground. Because the snake's body is so long, the head reaches about eye level with a standing human. The king cobra fixes its beady eyes on the person's face and opens its mouth to display its fierce fangs. It also hisses—and this noise is uniquely terrifying. Unlike most snakes, which make an airy sound when they hiss, the king cobra emits a low growl that sounds a bit like an angry dog.

In an attempt to make itself look larger and scarier, the king cobra also spreads the skin of its neck outward to form a hood. It does this by extending its flexible neck ribs, which work like the metal braces of an umbrella. The king cobra's hood is not as wide as those of some other cobra species, but it gets the point across. Anyone who sees this snake standing erect, hissing, with its neck flared, instantly understands the deadly danger that faces them.

A wise person will back away when faced with this display. If the king cobra feels that the threat is gone, it will sink back down to the ground and go on its way. If it is pushed just a little bit too far, though, the snake will strike. It uses its powerful body to propel itself forward, covering a gap of up to 7 feet (2 m) in an instant. It bites deep and holds on, pumping venom into its victim's flesh.

## A Deadly Bite

This bite delivers the highest venom load in the snake kingdom. The hollow fangs inject enough toxic liquid into the victim to kill up to twenty people—or, as has been seen on several occasions, one full-grown elephant. The elephant incidents have occurred in countries where elephants are used as working animals. While trampling through snake-infested underbrush, the elephants disturb resting cobras, which lash out to strike at the in-

# TOO HOT TO HANDLE

King cobras are well known for their use in snake-charming acts in some parts of the world. These serpents rise menacingly from baskets, spread their hoods, and sway to the sound of a snake charmer's flute, seeming to dance to the music. They appear to be hypnotized and utterly dominated by their human masters.

The situation, however, is not as controlled as it looks. It is true that king cobras get used to humans who handle them often and are less likely to strike these people. But a cobra can never be completely tamed. If startled or angered, even the most trusted king cobra will strike—and they often do. Most snake charmers are bitten at some point during their careers.

Smart handlers understand this danger and take steps to minimize it. They try to keep a safe distance from a dancing snake. In some cultures, snake charmers also receive weekly tattoos with venom-bearing ink. They believe that these tattoos work like vaccinations to protect them from the king cobra's bite. But smart snake charmers keep a supply of antivenom on hand, just in case. They know that when it comes to the king cobra, it is always better to be safe than sorry.

vading feet and legs. The unlucky bite victims often die, sometimes with shocking speed.

An account of one such attack illustrates this fact. In 1991 a timber crew in central India was hard at work when a king cobra rose from the grass and bit a work elephant on the knee. Immediately, says the account,

When the king cobra feels threatened, it rises up from the ground and flares the skin on its neck to form a hood. When it attacks, it bites deep and holds on—pumping deadly venom into its victim.

the elephant "trumpeted in agony and went berserk. It attacked everything standing, including other elephants. Much destruction resulted from its 20-minute rampage, after which it suddenly stopped, sank to its knees, and gently rolled over dead."[9] Due to the king cobra, this elephant's working days were unexpectedly over.

The king cobra's venom works just as quickly in humans. After being injected, the liquid immediately goes to work on the central nervous system, damaging the body's communication and control network. Meanwhile, severe pain and swelling develop in and around the bite site. The victim's vision becomes blurry, and he or she becomes dizzy and drowsy. The victim soon falls into a coma as the kidneys, heart, and lungs begin to fail. Without prompt treatment, he or she may soon die.

The likelihood of death depends on how much venom actually entered the person's system. King cobras do not always inject a killing dose of venom. In fact, sometimes they do not inject any venom at all. These dry bites are painful and frightening. But unless the puncture wounds become infected, a dry bite does not make its victim sick. Studies suggest that in human bite victims, dry bites occur around 40 percent of the time.

These odds are pretty good compared to some other snakes—but they are not good enough. The fact remains that about 60 percent of the king cobra's victims, if left untreated, will die a quick and painful death. This outcome is all too likely in the rural areas where king cobras are most likely to be found. When people live side by side with this killer, death is always lurking just around the corner.

# Chapter 5

# Dubois' Sea Snake

The vast majority of the world's three-thousand-plus snake species live on land. About sixty species, though, have adapted to a seagoing life. Found in warm coastal waters around the globe, sea snakes are a beautiful but deadly bunch. They are highly venomous—an important adaptation for a predator whose prey might just swim away if it does not die quickly.

All sea snakes are dangerous. But scientific tests have revealed that the Dubois' sea snake, which is named after the French naturalist Charles Frédéric Dubois, is by far the most venomous of the bunch. A mere .044 milligrams of its venom per kilogram (2.2 pounds) of body weight is enough to kill a human being. This lethal number ranks the Dubois' sea snake as the world's third most-venomous snake overall. In its ocean home, though, this snake is the undisputed champion. No potential prey is safe when this killer is on the hunt.

## Body Basics

The Dubois' sea snake is not a particularly large serpent. These reptiles are usually around 3 feet (.9 m) long, which is about the length of an adult human's leg. Especially large individuals can be up to 5 feet (1.5 m) long, but this is rare. The body is medium in build and compressed on both sides to form a prominent bony ridge down the back. The tail is also compressed to form a flat, fin-like keel. This feature is typical of sea snakes, which wave their tails back and forth to push themselves through the water.

In terms of color, the Dubois' sea snake is lightly patterned, with shades ranging from dark brown to tan. The scales are small to medium in size and are diamond shaped, with dark interiors and lighter outlines. The outlines are narrow on some of the scales and much wider on others, which creates a subtle striped pattern. This pattern is variable from snake to snake, appearing very dark in some individuals and very light in others.

The pattern breaks up at the snake's head, which is slightly wider than the body. Here the scales are irregular in shape and color. Rings of darker scales surround the snake's eyes, which are perfectly round with tan irises and black pupils. The mouth is small and so are the hollow fangs inside, which are typically less than .1 inches (.25 cm) long.

## Home and Habits

Like all snakes, the Dubois' sea snake is cold-blooded, which means it cannot regulate its own body temperature. It needs a warm environment to function. This is a greater challenge for sea snakes than for their land-living cousins since water whisks away body heat very quickly. To solve this problem, the Dubois' sea snake lives along the northern Australian coast in waters that stay warm year-round. It prefers shallow, sunny reefs but sometimes dives as deep as 260 feet (79 m).

A dive this deep only lasts a short time. Sea snakes are reptiles, not fish, and they need air to survive. They do not need to breathe as often as land snakes do because they have extra-large lungs and oxygen-absorbing skin—adaptations that have developed over millions of years of ocean living. Even with these features, though, the Dubois' sea snake must come to the surface periodically to suck in a new lungful of air.

*No prey is safe from the venomous Dubois' sea snake (pictured), which is found in the warm coastal waters of northern Australia. Its diamond-shaped scales range in shades from dark brown to tan.*

Between breaths, the reptile glides gracefully through its underwater home, using its strong, flattened tail to power itself forward. It may take shelter and rest inside seaweed, corals, and sponges during the midday hours and at night. It relaxes and waits until it is time to look for food.

## On the Hunt

The Dubois' sea snake is crepuscular, which means it is active at dawn and at dusk. It is most often seen hunting as night approaches. When the sun sinks below the horizon and the waters dim, this reptile emerges from its daytime hiding place to search for its evening meal. The menu usually includes eels and reef fish, including blennies, parrot fish, and surgeonfish.

To find these creatures, the snake looks around with its sharp eyes. It also feels vibrations in the water through its skin. Between its sight and its sense of touch, the Dubois' sea snake detects the signs of nearby prey. If no such signs are detected, the snake pokes its head into reef nooks and crannies to see if anything tasty is hiding inside. Its long, flexible body lets it enter any and every hole in search of prey.

Coral reefs are full of living creatures, so before long the Dubois' sea snake is likely to find a victim. The snake opens its jaws wide. It lunges, bites, and then backs off—but not too far. It keeps a close eye on the bitten prey as its venom goes to work. The venom, which contains a powerful neurotoxin, paralyzes the prey almost immediately and prevents any possibility of escape.

When the prey is helpless, just seconds after being bitten, the Dubois' sea snake moves in to begin its meal.

It eats the same way its land-based cousins do, starting at the prey's head and using its small, sharp teeth to pull the animal little by little into its body. Flexible jaw ligaments allow the snake to open its mouth much wider than its own body, if necessary, to swallow large prey. Soon the prey has been engulfed, and the snake can begin the process of digesting its food.

*The parrotfish (pictured) is a favorite meal of the Dubois' sea snake. To find its prey, the snake relies on its sharp eyesight and the vibrations it feels on its skin.*

# THE DUBOIS' SEA SNAKE AT A GLANCE

- **Scientific name:** *Aipysurus duboisii*
- **Scientific family: Elapidae**
- **Range: Coastal waters of northern Australia, Papua New Guinea, and New Caledonia**
- **Habitat: Shallow reefs**
- **Average size: 3 feet (.9 m)**
- **Diet: Fish and eels**
- **Life span: Unknown**
- **Key features: Diamond-shaped scales and flattened tail**
- **Deadly because: Potent, specialized venom**
- **Conservation status: Least concern**

## Specialized Venom

Compared to many other snakes, the Dubois' sea snake injects only a tiny amount of venom with each bite. A typical attack delivers less than one-thousandth the amount of venom injected by a king cobra. It is incredible that this venom is so potent in such small amounts.

But there is a reason for this quick-acting effect. The Dubois' sea snake is a specialized killer whose body has adapted over millions of years to hunt a very particular group of prey. Its venom has adapted to be particularly deadly to the eels and reef fish this serpent depends on for food. The snake's poison therefore attacks the prey's system with lethal efficiency.

# HELPLESS ON LAND

Sea snakes of all types are excellent swimmers, as one would expect from oceanic animals. They are much more agile in the water than their land-living cousins. They move quickly and gracefully through their underwater homes, and they can swim either forward or backward with equal ease.

These added swimming abilities, though, have come at a cost. Land snakes have specialized scales called scutes on their bellies that they use to grip and slither across the ground. Sea snakes lost these scales as they gained other features—and without scutes, they are virtually helpless on land. A beached Dubois' sea snake may be able to wriggle itself awkwardly back into the sea, if it is close enough to the waterline. If it is stranded far up the beach, though, it is stuck—and it is probably upset and ready to strike. Beachgoers should stay far away from these beautiful but deadly creatures.

This adaptation is unfortunate for the animals that are regularly hunted by the Dubois' sea snake. For other creatures, though, including humans, it is a major stroke of luck. Sea snake venom does not have the same effect on mammals, birds, and other non-ocean animals as it does on fish. This is not to say that it is not dangerous to people. It can and does affect humans and can even kill them. But a person who is bitten by the Dubois' sea snake will not suffer the same devastating effects that a fish would.

He or she will, though, experience some unpleasant effects. The fangs of the Dubois' sea snake are so small that a person may not even realize he or she has been bitten at first. Within about thirty minutes, though, the victim starts to feel stiff and achy all over as the snake's venom works to break down muscle tissue. Blurred vision, dizziness, and drowsiness develop next as the venom attacks the central nervous system. If the bite victim does not receive immediate treatment, the symptoms will progress and paralysis and respiratory failure may occur.

## Interaction with Humans

It is very uncommon for human swimmers to be bitten by the Dubois' sea snake. This reptile is not aggressive and does not try to bite people unless it is highly provoked. And even if the snake does bite, it does not always deliver venom. One reason is that the snake's fangs are too short to puncture a diver's wetsuit to reach the skin below. Unprotected swimmers who do receive skin punctures also have a good chance of avoiding the snake's venom since this serpent delivers dry bites an estimated 65 percent of the time.

Still, encounters with the Dubois' sea snake should not be taken lightly. These snakes can be deadly, especially on trawlers, where sea snakes of many species are often scooped up in nets along with fish and shrimp. Fishermen have the hazardous job of removing the snakes from the catch and tossing them back into the sea. The angry reptiles do not take kindly to this treatment. They will bite if they can—and serious injury and illness may be the result.

*The Dubois' sea snake (pictured) injects only a small amount of venom into its prey. That venom is extremely potent—especially to the eels and reef fish that the snake relies on for food.*

One of many incidents of this type occurred in July 2015, when a fisherman was bitten on the thumb while pulling a snake from a net. According to a hospital report, the man almost immediately became "giddy and breathless" and later developed neurological symptoms, including "drooping eyelids, difficulty in speaking, swallowing and breathing."[10] The man spent two days on a ventilator, unable to breathe on his own, before his condition finally started to improve.

Although fishermen are the most likely group to encounter sea snakes, beachgoers may come upon them as well. Dubois' sea snakes sometimes wash up, very much alive, on the shorelines of northern Australia. They pose a grave danger to curious walkers who try to get a too-close look. This creature may be beautiful and interesting, but when it comes to deadly predators like the Dubois' sea snake, it is always best to keep a safe distance.

# Chapter 6

# Reticulated Python

As the world's longest snake, the reticulated python is like something out of a nightmare. This serpent's body goes on and on, stretching out as long as a limousine. That is the length of five adult humans lying end to end. This is a terrifying sight—and potentially a fatal one as well. The reticulated python is a vicious and powerful hunter that can hunt and kill prey up to one-quarter of its own length. This means that people are definitely on the menu.

Despite its vast size, the reticulated python is not the world's heaviest snake. That honor goes to the anaconda, a shorter but chunkier serpent that can tip the scales at well over 500 pounds (227 kg). Pythons are usually less than half the weight of an anaconda of the same length. This weight difference, though, is part of what makes the reticulated python so dangerous. Leaner and meaner, the python is more active and aggressive than its heavier relative. It poses a deadly threat to any animal or person that enters its territory.

## Body Basics

The reticulated python gets its name from its colors. The word *reticulated* means "netlike," and it refers to the complex geometric patterns this snake bears on its skin. The specific patterns and colors vary greatly between individuals, but the back generally is marked with a series of irregular diamond-shaped blotches that range from brown to tan to yellow in color. The blotches are outlined in a darker color, making it look a bit like a net has been thrown over the snake's body. Smaller blotches in various colors line the snake's sides.

Together, all of these markings mimic the fallen leaves and dappled sunshine found in the snake's environment. They act as camouflage, making the python hard to see. This type of camouflage is known as disruptive coloration because it disrupts the animal's body outline. At a glance, other animals—and people—often do not notice the reticulated python basking on the ground.

This hiding ability is remarkable considering this snake's enormous size. Reticulated pythons regularly reach lengths over 20 feet (6 m) and weights of more than 200 pounds (91 kg). But they can get even bigger—*much* bigger. Over the past two hundred years, there have been many published reports of 30-foot-plus (9 m) monsters.

These reports may or may not be accurate. Although reticulated pythons of such staggering size may, indeed, have been spotted, they have not been measured carefully. This means no one can be certain of their true length. Officially, the largest-ever python is Medusa, a captive snake that lives in Kansas City, Missouri. When measured in October 2011, this reptile was found to be 25 feet (7.6 meters), 2 inches (5 cm) long, with a weight of 350 pounds (159 kg). Fifteen men had to stretch Medusa out to her full length in order for this measurement to be taken.

# Home and Habits

Captive pythons like Medusa can be found in zoos and other facilities all over the world. In the wild, though, reticulated pythons are limited to a much smaller range. These reptiles are native to Southeast Asia, from Indochina through the Philippines. They sometimes settle in woodlands and grasslands but strongly prefer tropical rain forests where average temperatures range from about 80° to 92°F (27° to 33°C). They are excellent swimmers and are often found near rivers, ponds, and other bodies of water.

Reticulated pythons are nocturnal. This means they are active during the night. They spend the daytime hours resting in trees or on the ground. Only when dusk arrives do they begin to stir. They open their round eyes, which are a striking deep orange with black, vertical slits for pupils. They look around for signs of prey.

Often there is no prey in sight, and the python decides to move to a better location. It moves off, heaving its bulk forward in a straight line rather than in a side-to-side motion. It does this by stiffening its ribs to provide support, then moving a set of belly scales forward to grip the ground and pull. By repeating this process over and over, the snake moves forward slowly, with a top speed of about 1 mile per hour (1.6 km/h). Little by little the snake makes its way across its territory.

# On the Hunt

As the reticulated python travels, it uses its sharp eyes to look for rustling grass and leaves that might hide prey. It flicks its forked tongue in and out of its mouth to col-

*The complex geometric patterns that mark the skin of the reticulated python (pictured) provide camouflage among fallen leaves and other features of its habitat. The ability to hide in plain sight is all the more remarkable given the snake's enormous size.*

lect scent particles from the air. It also uses heat-sensing pits on its jaw to detect the body heat of buried or hidden animals. Smaller pythons look mostly for signs left by small- to medium-size prey, such as rodents, monkeys, birds, and lizards. Larger pythons will pursue bigger prey, including wallabies, pigs, antelope, and even

# THE RETICULATED PYTHON
## AT A GLANCE

- Scientific name: *Python reticulatus*
- Scientific family: Pythonidae
- Range: Southeast Asia, including Indochina, Indonesia, and the Philippines
- Habitat: Tropical rain forests
- Length: Up to 30 feet (9 m)
- Diet: Mammals and birds
- Life span: Up to twenty-nine years
- Key features: Massive length
- Deadly because: Squeezes prey to death
- Conservation status: Vulnerable

leopards. As one expert explains, "Snakes are opportunists . . . they'll take whatever they can get."[11]

Eventually the python finds evidence that prey is nearby. When this happens, the python settles down and rests, still but alert. It watches and waits for prey to approach. It may wait on land, or it may enter a river or pond and lurk near the edge with just its eyes and nostrils showing.

If the python is lucky, an unwary animal will soon come too close—and when it does, the snake strikes. It shoots its large head forward with its jaws gaping open to reveal rows of long, curved, backward-pointing teeth. It bites the prey hard, driving its teeth deep into the flesh. The bite is not venomous and does not make the prey sick—but that does not matter. The python is much too big and powerful for most creatures to escape. Its strong jaws and buried teeth act like a vise grip to hold the prey tight.

As the snake's victim struggles helplessly, the python's mighty body springs into action. It coils itself around and around the prey. The number of coils depends on the size of the prey. The bigger the creature, the more coils the reticulated python will use to hold it tight.

*When it attacks, the reticulated python opens its jaws wide to reveal rows of long, curved, backward-pointing teeth. It bites down hard and deep so that the prey has no chance to escape.*

## Squeezed to Death

Once the prey is securely trapped, the snake starts to tighten its coils. This process is called constriction, and snakes that use it are called constrictors. The python squeezes harder and harder, crushing the life out of its prey.

Until recently, scientists believed that the reticulated python and other constrictors killed their prey by suffocation—squeezing them so tightly that they could not expand their lungs to get a breath. New studies, though, have found that this is not the case. Scientists now know that constriction puts so much pressure on the blood vessels that the heart can no longer push blood through the body. As a result, vital organs shut down within minutes.

The python is acutely aware of this process. It can feel its victim's heart hammering madly as it squeezes—and it also feels the heart faltering and then stopping. Only when the last spark of life disappears does the snake loosen its fatal grip and pull its teeth loose from the victim's body.

The python then shifts its body, bringing its head in line with the prey's head. It opens its mouth wide, stretching the ligaments of its jaws to create a vast, gaping maw. It slides the jaws around the prey's head and digs its teeth back into the flesh. Then it starts working its jaws back and forth—left, right, left, right. With each shift, the curved teeth pull the prey a little bit deeper into the python's throat. The prey slowly slides into the snake, forming a huge lump in the serpent's midsec-

# LIVING AMONG PYTHONS

In modern times, python attacks on humans are relatively rare. But interviews with the Agta tribe, a hunter-gatherer group that still lives alongside reticulated pythons in the Philippine rain forest, suggest that these animals hunt people just as enthusiastically as any other prey, if circumstances permit. A full 26 percent of the men in this six-hundred-member tribe say they have been attacked by pythons. Of these victims, fifteen had been bitten and eleven bore scars from their serpent encounters. The interviews also reveal that within a thirty-nine-year period, six tribespeople had been killed by pythons, including two children who were eaten by one very hungry snake on a single night.

This data suggests that reticulated pythons do not just attack people under rare, unusual conditions. They view humans as tasty treats and will eat them if they can. In short, these snakes are deadly predators that must be handled with care whenever human contact occurs.

tion. The snake then begins the process of digesting its prey, which may take anywhere from a few hours to ten weeks, depending on the size of the meal.

## Hungry for Humans

One snake expert recalls vividly the moment he almost became such a meal. The man was handling a dead rat near a large captive python when the snake got confused and struck. It dug its teeth into the keeper's forearm. Within three to five seconds, recalls the keeper, "He wrapped around my upper torso and

*Only the legs are visible as a reticulated python feeds on a deer. The python coils itself around its prey, squeezing so tightly that the animal's organs shut down. The snake then opens its mouth wide and slides its jaws around the head.*

neck. He was trying to get as many coils around me as he could. Once they get those coils around, it's just like a compactor; they just pull it tighter. I could still breathe, but it was hard. The pressure was unbelievable."[12]

The snake keeper was lucky. He managed to escape from the python by submerging its head under running water from a bathroom faucet, forcing it to release its grip when it opened its mouth to breathe. Others, however, have been less fortunate. The reticulated python is fully capable of subduing and eating human children and small adults, and it does so occasionally in its native areas. In 1995, for instance, a man named Ee Heng Chuan was squeezed to death by a 23-foot (7 m) reticulated python in southern Malaysia—and his case is just one of many. Reports of reticulated python attacks and fatalities have cropped up over and over for centuries in areas where this snake is known to roam.

In recent years many python incidents have involved captive snakes. It is legal to keep reticulated pythons as pets in many countries. These pets are spectacular but potentially deadly. People do not always realize that if their python escapes from its tank, it can attack and even kill its owners. One such incident occurred in 2008, when a Virginia woman died after being strangled by her pet python. Another incident took place in 2009, when a toddler narrowly escaped death after his mother attacked a constricting 18-foot (6 m) python with a knife. The wounded snake released the boy, who at that point was turning blue from oxygen loss.

These incidents prove that snakes do not have to be venomous to be deadly. The reticulated python cannot kill with a single bite, like some of its more feared relatives do, but people would be wise to take this creature seriously nonetheless. The reticulated python has all of the tools it needs to hunt and slay large animals. If humans get too close, they just may find that they end up on this deadly predator's menu.

# Source Notes

## Introduction: Feared but Fascinating

1. Quoted in *The Reptiles,* "Saving Snakes," Public Broadcasting Service, October 31, 2008. www.pbs .org.
2. Quoted in Clara Moskowitz, "Why We Fear Snakes," LiveScience, March 3, 2008. www.livescience.com.

## Chapter 1: Inland Taipan

3. Quoted in Dan Proudman and Stephanie Gardiner, "Snake-Bite Victim Could Have Been Dead in 45 Minutes," *Sydney Morning Herald Online*, September 28, 2012. www.smh.com.au.
4. Brandon Cornett, "Most Venomous Snake—Meet the Inland Taipan," Reptile Knowledge, 2015. www .reptileknowledge.com.

## Chapter 2: Black Mamba

5. Quoted in Duncan Guy, "The Man Who Loves Deadly Black Snakes," IOL SciTech, March 23, 2103. www .iol.co.za.
6. Quoted in *Telegraph,* "Student Dies After Being Bitten by Snake," December 13, 2011. www.telegraph .co.uk.

## Chapter 3: Saw-Scaled Viper

7. Quoted in Paul Bentley, "The Viper on My Drive: Gran Captured Deadly Foot-Long Snake from India

with Her Ice Tongs," *Daily Mail*, September 6, 2012. www.dailymail.co.uk.

## Chapter 4: King Cobra

8. Philip Seff and Nancy R. Seff, "King Cobra," *Our Fascinating Earth.* www.fascinatingearth.com.
9. Quoted in Science Heathen, "King Cobra." www.scienceheathen.com.

## Chapter 5: Dubois' Sea Snake

10. *Hindu,* "Man Bitten by Sea Snake Treated Successfully at GH," August 8, 2015. www.thehindu.com.

## Chapter 6: Reticulated Python

11. Quoted in Ker Than, "Strangulation of Sleeping Boys Puts Spotlight on Pythons," National Geographic News, August 6, 2013. www.news.nationalgeographic.com.
12. Quoted in Peter Martin, "To Be Constricted by a Python," *Esquire*, June 29, 2006. www.esquire.com.

**ambush:** A type of hunting in which the hunter hides and waits for prey to approach rather than actively pursuing prey.

**antivenom:** A medicine that counteracts the effects of snake venom. Also called antivenin.

**camouflage:** Colors or patterns that help an animal to blend into its surroundings.

**cold-blooded:** Having a body temperature that varies with the environment; unable to internally regulate body temperature.

**constriction:** Using the body to squeeze prey to death.

**constrictor:** A snake that uses constriction to kill prey.

**crepuscular:** Active mostly at dawn and dusk.

**dry bite:** A bite from a venomous snake that delivers no venom.

**habitat:** The natural home or environment of an animal.

**hood:** The spread neck flaps of a snake.

**keeled:** Having a raised ridge running down the center.

**nocturnal:** Active mostly during the nighttime.

**scutes:** Belly scales that help a snake to grip the ground and aid in slithering.

**sidewinding:** A method of locomotion that involves moving the body sideways and forward with a wavelike motion.

**strike:** The lunge a snake makes to deliver a bite.

**toxin:** A poisonous substance produced by a living thing.

**venom:** A poisonous liquid made by many creatures, including snakes, that is injected by biting or stinging.

# For Further Research

## Books

Leslie Anthony, *Snakebit*. Vancouver, Canada: Greystone, 2011.

Cindy Blobaum, *Awesome Snake Science! 40 Activities for Learning About Snakes*. Chicago: Chicago Review, 2012.

Discovery Channel, *Discovery Snakeopedia: The Complete Guide to Everything Snake*. New York: Liberty Street, 2014.

Dianna Dorisi-Winget, *Wild About Snakes: Pythons*. North Mankato, MN: Capstone, 2011.

Sara Latta, *Scared Stiff: Everything You Need to Know About 50 Famous Phobias*. San Francisco: Zest, 2014.

Chris Mattison, *Smithsonian Nature Guide: Snakes and Other Reptiles and Amphibians*. New York: Dorling Kindersley, 2014.

Mark Siddall, *Poison: Sinister Species with Deadly Consequences*. New York: Sterling Signature, 2014.

Marilyn Singer, *Venom*. Minneapolis: Millbrook, 2014.

## Websites

**Exotic Pets: Snakes** (www.exoticpets.about.com/od /snakes). Explore various snake-keeping topics on this informative site.

**Planet Deadly** (www.planetdeadly.com). If something is dangerous or deadly in any way, it is probably profiled on this site.

*Reptiles Magazine* (www.reptilesmagazine.com/Snakes). Including easy-to-access information on every aspect of snakes, this site is a serpent-lover's delight.

**Snake Attack** (www.newser.com/tag/29610/1/snake -attack.html). This page provides links to current news stories involving snake attacks around the world.

**Snaketype** (www.snaketype.com). Browse this site to find photos, facts, and information about many snake species.

# Index

Note: Boldface page numbers indicate illustrations.

importance of, 5

taipan. *See* inland taipan

venom
  of black mamba, 21,
    25
  of Dubois' sea snake,
    48, 53–55
  of inland taipan, 9, 14,
    33–35
  of king cobra, 38, 47
  medical uses of, 6–7
  milking of, **6**, **36**
  number of snake
    species with, 4
  of saw-scaled viper,
    33–35
viper. *See* saw-scaled
  viper

# Picture Credits

Cover: Thinkstock Images

6: © Tony Phelps/NPL/Minden Pictures

11: © Robert Valentic/NPL/Minden Pictures

13: © Roland Seitre/Minden Pictures

17: © Mick Tsikas/Reuters/Corbis

21: NPL/Minden Pictures

23: © Michael D. Kern/NPL/Minden Pictures

26: Karl H. Switak/ScienceSource

29: Christian Hütter/Newscom

32: © Robert Valentic/NPL/Minden Pictures

36: © Jeffrey L. Rotman/Corbis

40: Craig Burrows/Shutterstock.com

43: Surya99/Shutterstock.com

46: © Sanjeev Gupta/epa/Corbis

50: © Photoshot

52: Depositphotos

56: © Oceans-Image/Photoshot

61: © Ch'ien Lee/Minden Pictures

63: MikkoStig/REX/Newscom

66: © Miles Barton/NPL/Minden Pictures

# About the Author

Kris Hirschmann has written more than three hundred books for children. She owns and runs a business that provides a variety of writing and editorial services. She lives near Orlando, Florida, with her husband, Michael, and her daughters, Nikki and Erika.